CRASH!
BOOM!

A MATH TALE

Robie H. Harris   illustrated by Chris Chatterton

CANDLEWICK PRESS

Hmmmm . . .
1

Oh!
1 more.

Hey!

I want it to be as
tall as ME!

2 more?

It's up.

It's . . . a little . . . wobbly.

But it's up!

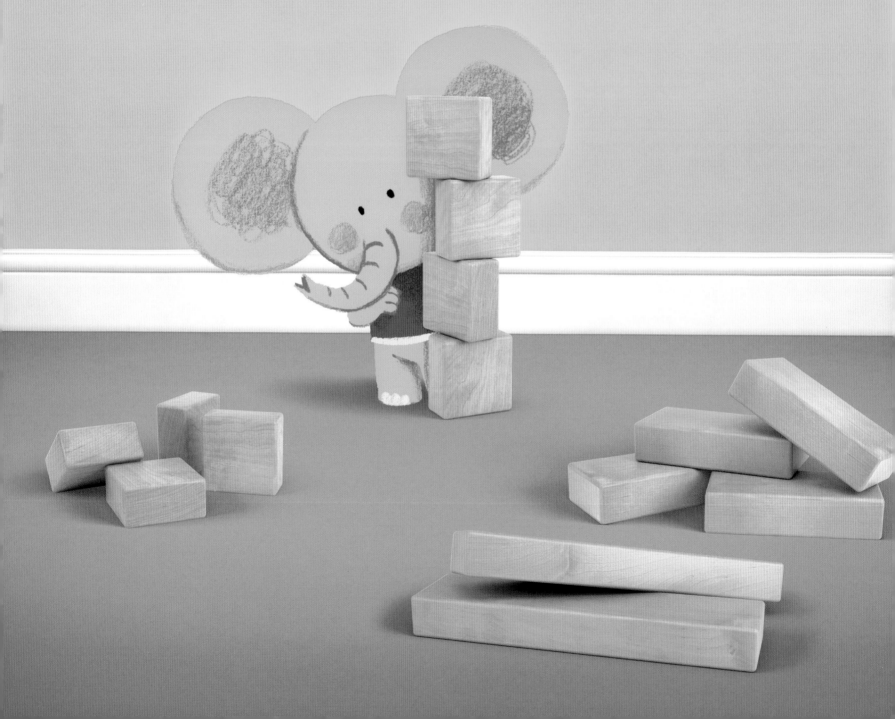

1 2 3 4

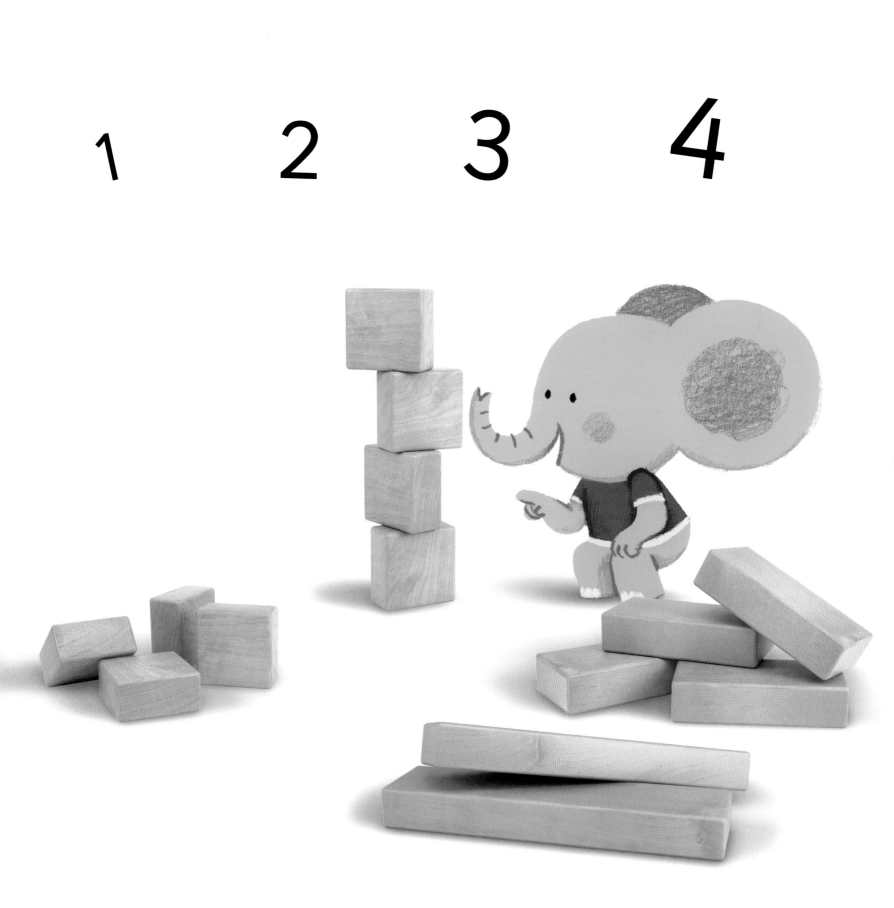

WOW!

I did it!

It's as tall as ME!

BOOM!

OH NO-OOO . . .

It's not tall anymore.
It's shorter than me.

It's down.

But it has to go up.

Not down!

It has to be as
tall as ME!

Hmmm . . .

Up?
Too wobbly.

Flat.
Maybe?

More?

Still not as tall as ME.

More.

Please . . . don't . . . fall.

4 5 6 7 8

WHOOPEE!
I did it!

It's not wobbly. It's still up.

It's as tall as ME!

So-ooo . . . CRASH!

BOOM!

Well, this time

I CRASH-BOOMED IT!

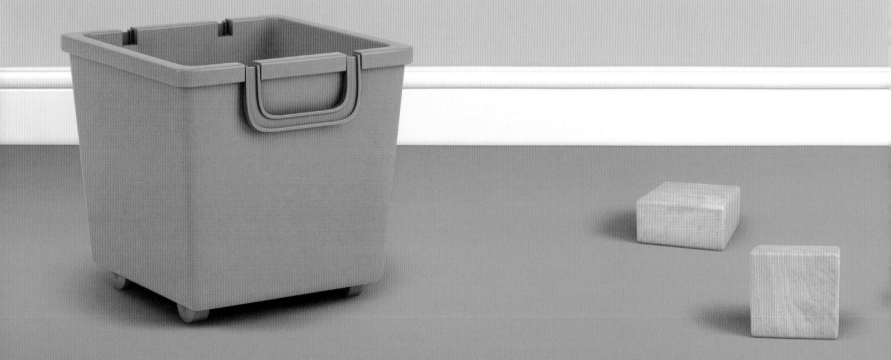

Hey . . .

What if?

Hmmmm . . .

Yep. Got it!

For "Block Builders" Rosie, Daisy, Ella, Sam, David, and Ben, for inspiring me to write this book. For Hal Melnick and David Harris, who shared their deep understanding of math and young children along with their expertise, insights, and criticism when responding to my nonstop queries. For Ellen Kelley, Emily Linsay, Bill Harris, Robyn Heilbrun, and Elizabeth Levy, for being there for all my on-the-spot questions.
R. H. H.

For Travis
C. C.

Thank you to everyone at Community Playthings for the beautiful wooden blocks you make with the utmost care and precision—blocks that allow children of all ages to wonder, explore, play, think, create, even fail, and finally to feel the pride of success, all while discovering endless math and science concepts.